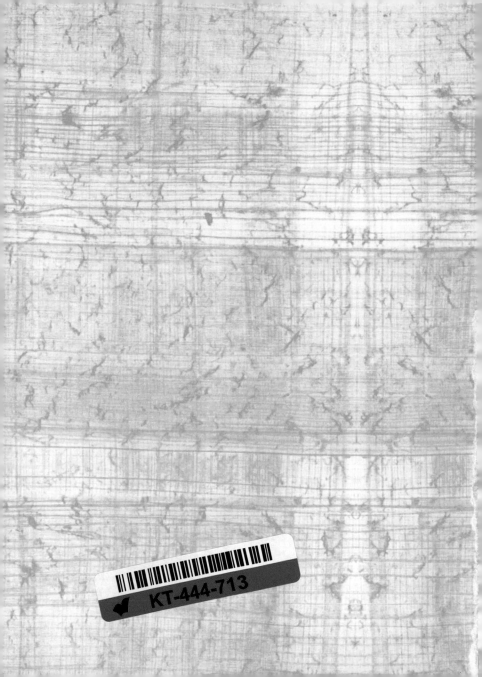

God's Precious Love
Copyright © 2002 by Zondervan
ISBN 0-310-98907-8

Compiler: Londa P. Alderink
Associate Editor: Janice Jacobson
Design Manager: Amy J. Wenger
Designer: Amy Peterman

All artwork is copyrighted by Joni Eareckson Tada.

Printed in China
02 03 04/HK/5 4 3 2 1

God's Precious Love

JONI
EARECKSON TADA

inspirio

The gift group of Zondervan

IF YOU'RE MEETING JONI FOR THE FIRST TIME...

Joni Eareckson Tada, as the result of a diving accident, has lived in a wheelchair, paralyzed from the shoulders down, for over thirty years. "So many actions, sensations, thoughts, and feelings were crowded into that fragment of time," Joni recalls about the accident. She continues, "I recall so clearly the details of those few dozen seconds—seconds destined to change my life forever. And there was no warning or premonition.

"What happened on July 30, 1967, was the beginning of an incredible adventure which I feel compelled to share because of what I have learned." And in a quest to better understand the goodness of God in the midst of suffering, she has invested most of the past thirty plus years in a probing and personal study of God's Word.

EXCESSIVE LOVE

*W*hen my husband Ken and I were dating, one word marked the expression of his love for me: Excessive. I received more vases of fresh yellow roses, stuffed animals, sweetheart-cards, and candies than I care to remember. I pleaded with him to lighten up, but I learned that not only is love blind, it's deaf. The next day I would receive pink roses instead of yellow ones. There are many more solid evidences of Ken's love I could point to, but it was the excesses that delighted me.

We never need doubt the love of Christ. We have plenty of solid evidence. But there may be times when we might wonder just how much Jesus delights himself in us. It is true that bearing the Father's wrath on the cross was the ultimate test of how immense Christ's love is, but our soul wants to know more. I want to know how passionately, how intensely he *feels* about me. Did Jesus desire to come to earth? Or was it a matter of fulfilling divine duty?

The question is answered in blood. There is a word that marks the love of Christ and that word is "excessive." His love for you overflows all reason, all expectations, all your hopes and dreams. For Christ to lay down his life for us says that his covenant is no schoolboy pledge. It emanates powerful emotion. For him to die for you, is for him to be delighted in you.

Our exultant and rapturously happy God loves you. He loves me. Frankly, I can't keep such good news to myself. When you're in love, one thing's for certain: you tell others about it. We are happier and more complete when we express our love for God to

those around us. Delight in God's love is incomplete unless it is expressed. As C.S. Lewis says, "We delight to praise God because our praise of his love not merely expresses, but it completes our enjoyment."

The point of this book is to ignite your praise for God and his excessive love for you. I've included lots of my favorite insights to fuel your thoughts. I want you to take time to enjoy the Lover of your soul. I want you to feel the overflow of his love for you, and I trust that as you slowly turn each page, you will express in words or song your love for our Savior.

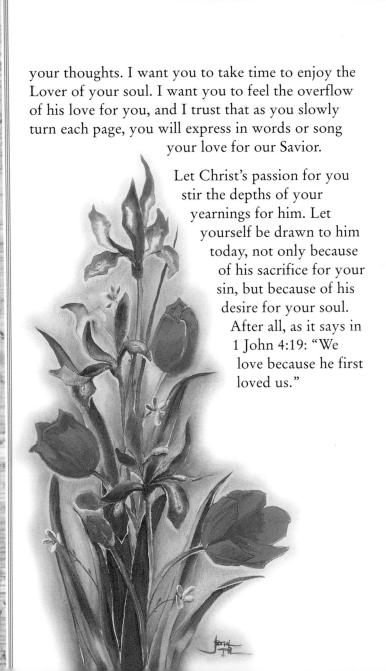

Let Christ's passion for you stir the depths of your yearnings for him. Let yourself be drawn to him today, not only because of his sacrifice for your sin, but because of his desire for your soul. After all, as it says in 1 John 4:19: "We love because he first loved us."

As we begin this book together, would you pray with me?

Lord Jesus, I am deeply moved by the extravagant, excessive display of your love for me. I am gripped by the intensity of your desire and emotion for my soul. You take delight in me, and my heart rises to take delight in you. Help me to ponder the excesses of your love. And help me to honor your love as I rise to a new level of trust, obedience, and confidence in you. In your precious name, Amen.

JONI EARECKSON TADA,
Artist and Author

THE APPLE OF HIS EYE

Keep me as the apple of your eye, O Lord;
hide me in the shadow of your wings.
PSALM 17:8

Who's the apple of your eye? Your grandchild? Your son recently promoted?
Your fiancée with those soft eyes and that tender
smile? Whoever is the apple of your eye, one thing's
for certain: you love that individual with a fervent
and intense love. That person gives you joy
indescribable. In short, you *feel* something for this
loved one.

You are the apple of God's eye. God feels powerful
emotions when it comes to you—God's love makes
him sing and rejoice over you. But why are you so
special to him? Why do you hold his affections?

First, when it comes to you, his joy is not merely
satisfaction over something you do, as though you
had him wrapped around your little finger with that
winsome way of yours. God's joy is in his own
goodness and wisdom, in the beautiful character of
his Son, and in the complexity and wonder of all that
he has made. His is not a complacent, lazy joy—his is
flying colors of victory; and the bone-tired, soot-
faced, grinning hero carrying the child to safety from
the burning building. In short, God's joy for you is
connected with something wonderful *he* has done.

God's joy and delight over you finds its best expression at the cross: "God so loved the world that he gave his one and only Son" (John 3:16). And he watched his Son die because he loves you. This means his joy and deep emotion for you is rugged, hard-won, and victorious. He is the admiral flying colors of victory over you. He's the hero who has carried you to safety. He is the joy-filled warrior who as brought you home. You are the apple of his eye.

Help me to remember, Lord, that your joy over me is pure and perfect and rooted in the way you love your Son. I can hardly believe that you actually feel something deep, powerful, and joyful when it comes to me—and it's all because of Jesus. Thank you for making me the apple of your eye. Amen.

TAKING
THE INITIATIVE

We love because God first loved us.
I JOHN 4:19

*I*t's a good thing I can't knot my hands into a fist. Because if I could, I'd probably punch things when I get mad. Ken, for instance. Wait—don't take me too seriously. I doubt our disagreements would ever get furious. But my husband and I are like every other couple you meet. We argue ... carefully observing a couple of basic rules, like letting the other person have his say without interrupting and promising to listen. Yet even when we argue with the best of intentions, we *still* come up against barricades.

When Ken and I reach an impasse, we sometimes sit for long minutes in belligerent silence. And as I sit there, I secretly resent the demands of marriage. I find I have a reluctance to give away any more than absolutely necessary. I feel a temptation to pull back from the full intensity of my relationship with Ken and settle for the "basic requirements."

But in the middle of all that stubbornness, Ken is usually the first to break the silence and take the initiative. Unaccountably, he will begin to show forgiveness and love. That *shocks* me. It catches me up short. Ken doesn't wait until I am repentant and promise to change my ways. He loves me ... argumentative person that I sometimes am. And that makes me love him all the more right back.

That's exactly what God has done for us. The Father didn't wait around until He had an apology before He sent Jesus. He took the initiative. He didn't fold his arms and tap His foot waiting until we "came around," until we shaped up and changed our ways.

No, God caught us up short in that "while we were yet sinners, Christ died for us" (Romans 5:8). I can't resist such love. It amazes me that the Lord loved me long before I promised to give Him my life or change my ways. The result is just as the apostle John predicted: I find that I love Jesus Christ "because he first loved us."

That's called taking initiative!

ive thanks to the LORD, for he is good; his love endures forever.

PSALM 107:1

his is love: not that we loved God, but that he loved us and sent his Son as an atoning sacrifice for our sins. Dear friends, since God so loved us, we also ought to love one another. No one has ever seen God; but if we love one another, God lives in us and his love is made complete in us.

1 JOHN 4:10-12

*Every good and perfect gift is from above, coming
down from the Father of the heavenly lights,
who does not change.*

JAMES 1:17

God is the author of every good and noble thing
in the world. All of the love, kindness, sharing
and forgiveness that one person has ever shown
to another comes ultimately from him.

"OH, JOY!"

"As a bridegroom rejoices over his bride, so will your God rejoice over you" (Isaiah 62:5). That's stupendous. Incredible. There aren't enough adjectives to describe the wonder.

*M*ay our Lord Jesus Christ himself and God our Father, who loved us and by his grace gave us eternal encouragement and good hope, encourage your hearts and strengthen you in every good deed and word.

2 THESSALONIANS 2:16-17

THE LORD IS GOOD

The LORD is good and his love endures forever;
his faithfulness continues through all generations.
PSALM 100:5

*J*t was a dull Saturday. My spirits were
drooping, and it was all I could do to fight off
depression. [My support brace] riding high was
digging into my ribs, forcing me to draw deep
breaths now and then. And when I did, I would say,
"The Lord is good." Somewhere after the fifth
"Lord is good," my friend turned and gave a good-
natured dig, asking, "What are you doing? Trying to
convince yourself?"

"You've got it," I replied. It's not that I doubted
God's goodness; I simply wanted to remind my dry
cracked soul of the truth. David, the psalmist, often
grabbed his innermost being by the scruff of the
neck, demanding, "Why are you downcast, O my
soul? Why so disturbed within me? Put your hope

in God, for I will yet praise him, my Savior and my God" (Psalm 42:5-6). It's easy to announce God's goodness when your spirits are soaring; it's another thing a more God—glorifying thing—to proclaim the goodness of God out loud when you're under the weather.

Lord, you are so good and your love is everlasting. Help me to be an extension of that same love and grace for others.

EVERLASTING LOVE

The LORD did not set his affection on you and choose you because you were more numerous than other peoples, for you were the fewest of all peoples. But it was because the LORD loved you and kept the oath he swore to your forefathers.
DEUTERONOMY 7:7-8

*E*ver look in the mirror and think, *Ugh?* I have. In fact, I've held a mirror up to my soul at times and thought the same. *God, how can you stand me? I'm fickle, lazy, and prone to turn my back on you, given half a chance.*

This is why I love Deuteronomy 7:7-8. It's so comforting. There is nothing in you or me to attract or prompt the affections of God. The love of, let's say, one person for another is because of something in that other. But the love of God is free and spontaneous. God has loved you and me from everlasting; nothing in us can be the cause of what is already found in God from eternity. Second Timothy 1:9 explains that God "has saved us and called us to a holy life—not because of anything we have done but because of his own purpose and grace. This grace was given us in Christ Jesus before the beginning of time."

Here is the good news: God loved us when we were loveless, and this means his love is completely uninfluenced by us. His love comes barreling at us at full speed in a direct line, with all its force undiminished and undaunted; he has as much love for us as he has for the most godly of saints. God loves us the way he loves his Son, Jesus. Amazing love! How can it be?

Since your love for me has no beginning, Lord, that means it has no ending. It says in the Bible, "God is love" and "God is everlasting." How comforting to know that I will forever bask in your love.

*T*o each one of us grace has been given as Christ apportioned it.

EPHESIANS 4:7

*T*o those who have been called, who are loved by God the Father and kept by Jesus Christ: Mercy, peace and love be yours in abundance.

JUDE 1:1-2

*B*ecause of the LORD'S great love
we are not consumed,
for his compassions never fail.
They are new every morning;
great is your faithfulness.

LAMENTATIONS 3: 22-23

LOVE DISPLAYED

Who shall separate us from the love of Christ? Shall trouble or hardship or persecution or famine or nakedness or danger or sword? ... No, in all these things we are more than conquerors through him who loved us. For I am convinced that neither death nor life, neither angels nor demons, neither the present nor the future, nor any powers, neither height nor depth, nor anything else in all creation, will be able to separate us from the love of God that is in Christ Jesus our Lord.

ROMANS 8:35, 37-39

"This is a verse I'm *supposed* to believe," we say with a sigh, full of doubts. It sounds more like theological doctrine than practical reality, especially when we are the ones facing trouble, hardship, danger, or sword. But the apostle—who, incidentally, suffered a lot more than persecution or famine—wrote this sweeping statement specifically for those who would doubt the love of God in the midst of hardships.

Look at the last eleven words: "the love of God that is in Christ Jesus our Lord." If ever we are tempted to doubt God's good intentions, if ever he seems to be an uncaring deity sequestered in an ivory tower untouched by pain, we must remember the love of God *that is in Christ.* Christ who bore the weight of sin, the sting of spit, the bite of the whip, the accusations of ignorance, and the sufferings of the world. This is love poured out like wine, as strong as fire.

Lord, help me to better understand the strength and depth of your love. And Lord, help me to never take it for granted.

This is how we know what love is: Jesus Christ laid down his life for us.

1 JOHN 3:16

The LORD said:
"I have loved you with an everlasting love;
I have drawn you with loving-kindness."

JEREMIAH 31:3

*J*esus, Thy boundless love to me
    No thought can reach, no tongue declare;
        O, knit my thankful heart to Thee,
And reign without a rival there!
Thine wholly, Thine alone, I'd live,
Myself to Thee entirely give.

PAUL GERHARDT, TRANSLATED BY CHARLES WESLEY

The LORD your God is with you,
he is mighty to save.
He will take great delight in you,
he will quiet you with his love,
he will rejoice over you with singing.

ZEPHANIAH 3:17

Imagine. God rejoices over you and me with an actual melody. What's more, he quiets us with his loving song.

When a beautiful hymn keeps rolling over and over in my mind, its tune lifts my spirits. The song, I'm convinced is God's melody to me direct from his heart. He is rejoicing over me with singing. And all I need to do is listen and be inspired.

Jesus prayed, "Now this is eternal life: that they
may know you, the only true God, and Jesus Christ,
whom you have sent."
JOHN 17:3

How can we know God's love? We can know it when we look at the love of His Son, Jesus Christ. And we can understand mercy and compassion when we look at the way Jesus demonstrated it.

THE REAL SPECTACLE

When I consider your heavens,
the work of your fingers, O Lord,
the moon and the stars,
which you have set in place,
what is man that you are mindful of him,
the son of man that you care for him?
PSALM 8:3-4

I heard on the news that the Hubble telescope discovered a powerful, new megastar. Not only is it one hundred million times brighter than our sun, but also, to the astonishment of astronomers, it is in our own Milky Way galaxy. A thick cloud of gas and cosmic dust has hidden the star from our view all this time. It makes me look at the night sky a little differently. *And to think, Lord, that you created all these constellations with a snap of your fingers.* His fingers? It sounds so easy. According to Psalm 8:3, it is.

Thousands of years ago, David looked out on the stars he could see without the aid of Hubble and marveled, "What is man that you are mindful of him?"(Psalm 8:4). The ancient shepherd king knew nothing of the actual vastness of space, of far-flung galaxies blazing with the light of billions of suns too distant to be marveled at by earthbound men and women—but he knew of something even more marvelous and astounding. He knew of his Creator's love for humankind! To David, that was the *real* spectacle. It still is.

LOVE LIFTED ME

Souls in danger look above, Jesus completely saves;
He will lift you by his love out of the angry waves;
He's the Master of the sea, billows will obey;
He your Savior wants to be, be saved today.
Love lifted me! Love lifted me!
When nothing else could help, love lifted me!

I enjoy singing hymns. Hardly a day goes by that I don't stop whatever I'm doing, open a hymnal with a friend, and sing a few stanzas. But hey, I don't have to stop what I'm doing. Sometimes I keep doing what I'm doing and sing. But the hymns always make me thankful—and sometimes they help me express thanks.

Once when I was a speaker at a conference, I encountered a bunch of steps leading to a meeting room. With no ramp I was stuck. Well, not really. We flagged down four strong guys and gave them

instructions about where to hold the wheelchair.
As they carried me, I sang a thank you hymn to
them, "Love Lifted Me." And I meant it. Love that
is put into practice always gives us a lift. Love with
its sleeves rolled up, with muscle behind it, love that
looks for a need and rushes to meet it, love that
does something—that's the kind of love that
ministers most. That's the sort of love the Lord
Jesus has for us.

THINKING THE BEST

Love does not delight in evil but rejoices with the truth.
I CORINTHIANS 13:6

The scene of the crime was a disability rights conference. Actually, the real crime scene was the handicap stall in the ladies' rest room. I was rambling on to my friend, but I should have kept my opinions to myself. After all, we were in a public rest room. And—yikes!—one of the ladies beyond the closed door was the individual with whom I had a difference of opinion.

When my friend and I exited the stall, I came face-to-face with that lady. Thankfully, her face was lit up with laughter. "Gotcha!" she said good-naturedly. "I'm assuming you were about to come back to the table to tell me your opinion, right?"

I was as red as a watermelon. "Right," I said, relieved.

This woman demonstrated grace. I deserved a good scolding, but instead she believed the best of me. Don't you love it when people think the best of you? You say something stupid but your friend discounts it. She doesn't hold anything against you, and she even chooses to think the best. Now, that's grace.

God expresses that kind of grace, too. He doesn't hold anything against you; he thinks the best. If ten different interpretations could be made of a thing, with nine of them bad and one good, God's grace will take the good one and leave the other nine.

Lord, sometimes I forget how graciously you overlook my shortcomings and outright wrongdoings. Thank you for thinking the best of me and loving me in such a special way. Teach me to extend that kind of grace to others in your name.

The LORD longs to be gracious to you; he rises to show you compassion. For the LORD is a God of justice. Blessed are all who wait for him!

ISAIAH 30:18

*B*ecause of his great love for us, God, who is rich in mercy, made us alive in Christ.

EPHESIANS 2:4-5

*F*rom the fullness of God's grace we have all received one blessing after another.

JOHN 1:16

*I*f we confess our sins, God is faithful and just and will forgive us our sins and purify us from all unrighteousness.

1 JOHN 1:9

*R*omance is fleeting, but love is long.
Romance is flying, but love is a safe landing.
Romance seeks perfection, but love forgives faults.
Romance anguishes as it waits for the phone to ring
to bring a voice that says sweet things,
but love is the anguish of waiting for a call
that assures you someone else is safe and happy,
Romance is suspense, anticipation and surprise,
but love is dependability.
Romance is dancing in the moonlight, gazing deep into desired eyes,
But love is saying, "You're tired, honey, I'll get up this time."
Romance is delicious, but love nourishes.

ANONYMOUS

*Lord, I can see that you have this kind of love
for me. Help me to lose myself in loving You and
others in this way also. May I move past romance
and begin laying my life down ... in love.*

We know and rely on the love God has for us. God is love. Whoever lives in love lives in God, and God in him.

1 JOHN 4:16

O THE DEEP, DEEP LOVE OF JESUS

O the deep, deep love of Jesus,
vast, unmeasured, boundless, free!
Rolling as a mighty ocean
in its fullness over me!
Underneath me, all around me,
is the current of thy love
Leading onward, leading homeward
to thy glorious rest above!

O the deep, deep love of Jesus,
spread his praise from shore to shore!
How he loveth, ever loveth,
changeth never, nevermore!
How he watches o'er his loved ones,
died to call them all his own;
How for them he intercedeth,
watcheth o'er them from the throne!

O the deep, deep love of Jesus,
love of every love the best!
'Tis an ocean full of blessing,
'tis a haven giving rest!
O the deep, deep love of Jesus,
'tis heaven of heavens to me;
And it lifts me up to glory,
for it lifts me up to thee!

SAMUEL TREVOR FRANCIS

NO ONE CARES
AS JESUS CARES

Cast all your anxiety on Jesus because he cares for you.
1 PETER 5:7

Whether you are weak or strong, saintly or struggling, Jesus cares for you. I realize that you may be thinking, "Sure, Jesus cares for me in the general sense, as for the whole world, but when it comes to specifics surely there must be others He is more interested in. After all, I can't pray out loud ... I have a hard time understanding the Bible ... I can't seem to shake bad habits. Yes, I know He cares but not as much as He does for more obedient types."

Not so. The Lord's care for you does not hinge on your hang-ups. His care for you has nothing to do with you baggage of personal problems. You could be a wimp when it comes to standing for the Lord,

always getting distracted by everyday pressures. It doesn't matter. As a child of God, you matter. For you, dear believer, have the full force and undivided attention of eternal Love. Love that cares with no strings attached.

What other friend is there who thinks about you every moment, every second of the day and night? Truly, no one ever cared for you as Jesus cares!

You are always thinking of me and watching everything that concerns me. I love You, Jesus!

JESUS, MY FRIEND

A friend loves at all times.
PROVERBS 17:17

*Oh the comfort, the inexpressible comfort of feeling safe
with a person. Having neither to weigh words nor
measure thoughts but pouring them all out like chaff and
grain together—certain that a faithful hand will keep
what is worth keeping, and with a breath of kindness,
blow the rest away.*
GEORGE ELIOT

*J*f you have a friend like that, you have a
treasure. Someone with whom you can peel
back the layers of your heart, knowing that he or
she will handle tenderly and loyally everything
that's revealed.

That's why I consider Jesus to be my friend. Of
course, there used to be times in prayer when I
would get tongue-tied over whether or not I was

praising Him properly. I would measure far too carefully my words, wondering if my prayer was progressing the way it should in a tidy order of adoration, confession, thanksgiving, and supplication. Sometimes I just gave up in frustration.

All the while, Jesus must have been waiting for me to simply peel back the layers of my heart and openly share a tumble of thoughts and confessions, like chaff and grain. He wanted to assure me that with His faithful hand He would keep what was worth keeping in my prayer and gently blow the rest away.

GOD'S GOODNESS: OUR RESPONSE

Last Easter, like most of you, I read through the story of the crucifixion to prepare my heart for Easter morning. And I found myself deliberating over the words of Christ when He cried in anguish from the cross, "My God, my God, why have you forsaken me?"

I have to admit it. The idea that the Father would allow His Son to suffer the torture of crucifixion is beyond me. The humiliation of nakedness, the searing pain, the agony of tears, the spit of drunken soldiers, the scorn of a jeering mob. As tears mingled with blood on His battered face, Jesus cried out to His Father—the One who had not once turned away from Him in all of eternity.

The reply was silence. Cold, accusing silence.

Heaven itself accused Jesus of sins in those horrible moments: lusting and lying, cheating and coveting, murder and hypocrisy, cruelty and deceit. Of course, Christ had never been guilty of any of those sins, *but we are.* And every one of our sins was racked up on His account right there on that cross, as the prophet Isaiah testified in Isaiah 53:4-6 and as Paul wrote in Colossians 2:13-15.

So where was God's goodness in treating Christ so? Where was the Father's kindness in turning His back on His only Son— while Jesus cried out in horror and grief?

On that terrible, wonderful day, God's goodness and kindness were directed toward you. God forsook His own Son ... so that He would never have to forsake you! And because of those dark hours two thousand years ago, God can say to me, "I will never leave you, Joni. I will never forsake you."

To think that God's anger for my sins was poured out on Christ—and that He has no anger left for me!

You know what that makes me want to do? Praise Him. Thank Him. Honor Him. Obey Him with all my heart and soul and mind. Unlike Christ, I will never have to agonize over separation from my Father. And neither will you. God poured the full measure of His wrath—the terrors of eternal hell—on His own Son ... so that you and I could be adopted into His very family. That's how much He loves you. And me.

*G*od so loved the world that he gave his one and
only Son, that whoever believes in him
shall not perish but have eternal life.

JOHN 3:16

I STAND IN AWE

You are beautiful beyond description,
Too marvelous for words,
Too wonderful for comprehension—
Like nothing ever seen or heard.

Who can grasp your infinite wisdom?
Who can fathom the depths of your love?
You are beautiful beyond description,
Majesty enthroned above.

And I stand, I stand in awe of you.
I stand, I stand in awe of you,
Holy God to whom all praise is due,
I stand in awe of you.

MARK ALTROGGE

God reaches down to embrace us, to kiss us on the forehead and tell us, "I love you" and "I love you" is a pretty accurate translation of the words God spoke through the Cross.
KEN GIRE

I kneel before the Father, from whom his whole family in heaven and on earth derives its name. I pray that out of his glorious riches he may strengthen you with power through his Spirit in your inner being, so that Christ may dwell in your hearts through faith. And I pray that you, being rooted and established in love, may have power, together with all the saints to grasp how wide and long and high and deep is the love of Christ, and to know this love that surpasses knowledge—that you may be filled to the measure of all the fullness of God.

ROMANS 3:14-19

HE FINISHES
WHAT HE STARTS

I will praise you, O LORD, with all my heart;
*   before the "gods" I will sing your praise.*
I will bow down toward your holy temple
*   and will praise your name*
*   for your love and your faithfulness,*
for you have exalted above all things
*   your name and your word.*
When I called, you answered me;
*   you made me bold and stouthearted.*
May all the kings of the earth praise you, O LORD,
*   when they hear the words of your mouth.*
May they sing of the ways of the LORD,
*   for the glory of the LORD is great.*
Though the LORD is on high, he looks upon the lowly,
*   but the proud he knows from afar.*
Though I walk in the midst of trouble,
*   you preserve my life;*
you stretch out your hand against the anger of my foes,
*   with your right hand you save me.*
The LORD will fulfill his purpose for me;
*   your love, O LORD, endures forever—*
*   do not abandon the works of your hands.*

PSALM 138

God always finishes what he starts. He never begins a project only to leave it half-done. He never walks away from a messy workbench. Unlike us, God never carries over items on his "To Do" list from one eternity to the next. He always completes what he begins. That includes you.

He started working on you years ago. Take heart that the blueprint for your life is till spread before him. He won't stop working on you until he reaches his goal.When reading Psalm 138, you can see how God accomplishes his work in your life. He fulfills his purpose in you with love and faithfulness (v.2). Part of his goal is to make you fearless and stout-hearted (v.3), humble (v.6), and confident in his ability to preserve and protect you (v.7). And he won't give up until he's done (v.8). He will never abandon or forsake you. His goal is to make you more like Jesus. And he won't stop working on his goal for you until you are complete.

Wow! I'm amazed at your love for me, Lord Jesus—your true love for me. Thank you for your abundant grace and kindness.

GOD'S LIFELONG CARE

"Even to your old age and gray hairs
I am he, I am he who will sustain you.
I have made you and I will carry you;
I will sustain you and I will rescue you," says the Lord.

ISAIAH 46:4

In one short sentence God promises that he will rescue, carry and sustain you. How? At least six times, God uses the personal pronoun to point to himself. His promises are signed, sealed and delivered on the basis of who he is. And he is faithful. He is loving. He rescues and carries you. It's a promise.

Lord, I don't live on reasons why. I live on
your promises. Draw me to them today and
help me to lean on your loving faithfulness.

*Y*et I am always with you; you hold me by my
    right hand.
*You guide me with your counsel, and afterward you will
    take me into glory.*
*Whom have I in heaven but you? And earth has nothing
    I desire besides you.*
*My flesh and my heart may fail, but God is the strength
    of my heart and my portion forever.*

PSALM 73:23-24, 26

GRANDMA GRACE

Jesus Christ is the same yesterday and today and forever.
HEBREWS 13:8

When I travel with my friends, Bev and Francie, we always enjoy heading back to our hotel room after a busy day of appointments and speaking engagements. We put on our pajamas, pile into bed together, and open up the Bible for devotions.

One evening it was Francie's turn to lead the hymns and Scripture reading. She rummaged through her suitcase and brought out an old, tattered Bible. "This is my Grandma Grace's," she smiled as she snuggled between Bev and me.

Francie cracked open the old Bible. The binding was torn, and she carefully turned each delicate page. Francie tilted the book so we could read Grandma Grace's faded scribbles in the margin. In old-fashioned

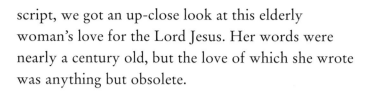

script, we got an up-close look at this elderly woman's love for the Lord Jesus. Her words were nearly a century old, but the love of which she wrote was anything but obsolete.

As Francie read aloud her grandmother's personal notes, I felt as though this woman shared the rhythm of my heart. We were kindred spirits. We could have been best friends. And her notes weren't reminiscent of dusty days gone by, for each word was a powerful and poignant reminder that Jesus is the same yesterday, today, and forever.

There's nothing old or worn out about the love of God. His love has not yellowed with age. It is neither fragile nor ragged at the edges. God's love is as current now as it was a century ago, as fresh today as it will be tomorrow.

Jesus, I'm amazed that You never change. You are always faithful. Your promises are time-tested. Together with the saints of the ages, including Grandma Grace ... I praise You!

I will sing of your strength, in the morning I will sing of your love; for you are my fortress, my refuge in times of trouble.
O my Strength, I sing praise to you; you, O God, are my fortress, my loving God.

PSALM 59:16-17

Trust in the LORD with all your heart
and lean not on your own understanding;
in all your ways acknowledge him,
and he will make your paths straight.

PROVERBS 3:5-6

An important truth is this: A loving, sovereign God can bring hope and beauty out of seemingly hopeless situations. He is worthy of our trust.

The LORD is a refuge for the oppressed, a stronghold in times of trouble.

PSALM 9:9

It's a crazy world. We keep crazy schedules. Life speeds by at a blur. Waves of circumstance roll over us, overwhelm us, threaten to drag us under. Yet God is with us, no matter where we find ourselves in life—right in the middle of the craziness. And anywhere, at any time, we may turn to him. Walk with him. Talk to him. Hear his voice. Feel his hand. And catch—even if just for a moment—a fragrance of heaven. He is our place of refuge, and this crazy world can never take that refuge away.

God has poured out his love into our hearts.
ROMANS 5:5

*T*he love that we need is God himself coming into our hearts. When the soul is perfected in love, it has such a sense of love that it can rest in it for eternity.
Andrew Murray

*L*ove is the greatest thing God can give us; for he himself is love.

JEREMY TAYLOR

*L*ove is more than a characteristic of God; it is his character.

ANONYMOUS

God is love.
1 JOHN 4:8

THE GOD WHO SEES

The eyes of the LORD are everywhere.
PROVERBS 15:3

*H*ow awesome to think that the living God sees us—every moment of every day. Even when we feel rejected, turned away or cast aside, our Lord sees which way we turn, and he calls to us in a barren and lonely place when we come to the end of ourselves. Others may overlook us; even those closest to us may not understand our heartache and disappointment. But there is One who does understand. There is one who does see. There is One who reaches out to us in our self-imposed exile and calls us to himself.

The God of the Universe sees me! Lord, I'm absolutely in awe that you not only see the outside of me, but you also see the inside. You know my innermost thoughts and feelings ... you know when I'm hurting, you know when I'm happy, you know when I need the touch of your gentle hand the most. Lord, thank you for caring about me so intimately.

WHO HELPS THE MOST?

The greatest of these is love.
1 CORINTHIANS 13:13

*P*eople often ask me, "Who helped you the most when you were hurting?"

That's a good question, but I can never seem to come up with a fast answer. I guess that's because there was no one person—no famous writer, no brainy seminary student, no super-sensitive counselor.

No, answers to my questions didn't come from "extraordinary" people. Frankly, when I was first injured in my diving accident and left paralyzed, I wasn't *looking* for wisdom or knowledge.

At first I was just looking for love.

That should be good news to those of you looking for ways to alleviate the pain of a friend in the hospital or a family member going through a crushing disappointment. If you and I are truly looking for an answer to the question, "How do I help those who are in pain?" we don't have to have a lot of answers. We don't even have to know all the specialized scriptures or a hundred and one reasons why God allows suffering. All we've got to know is love. The only Scripture we might need at first is 1 Corinthians 13.

I most appreciated those people who came into the hospital armed with love—and *Seventeen* magazines and Winchell's doughnuts. I appreciated them dropping by to help me write letters or to bring me writing paper and envelopes—even stamps. I was super-impressed when others bought birthday cards for me to send to a friend whose special day was coming up. I especially remember a few girls who made it a weekly ritual to come by and do my nails. What fun!

These were people who helped. They weren't trained counselors. They weren't spiritual giants. They weren't biblical wizards. They weren't Ph.D.'s. They weren't even full of all kinds of knowledge and wisdom. They were just commonplace, everyday sorts of people who gave me what I needed most of all ... God's love in action.

ear friends, let us love one another, for love comes from God. Everyone who loves has been born of God and knows God.
Whoever does not love does not know God, because God is love.

1 JOHN 4:7-8

GRACE

*G*race is what beauty looks like when it moves. God's grace is what he looks like when he moves, acting out his will through us.

Those on whom God's grace rests are truly gracious. They are truly beautiful. The cerebral palsied young man who smiles despite a dreary existence in a nursing home. The elderly woman who always seems to think of others rather than her aches and pains. The mother of two toddlers who is happy to baby-sit the neighbor's little boy. The pastor and his wife who take in a homeless couple for a week while they look for lodging. These people shine with a hint of glory. They shine because of God's grace.

Grace is God's energy—all bright, beautiful and full of power. And grace is most beautiful when God is moving through us to touch the lives of others who hurt.

*Lord, you are a gracious and loving God. Thank
you for the people in my life that live out your example.
Please help me to be gracious and loving in return.*

I know not what may come today,
Some needy soul may cross my way,
Lord give me words of cheer, I pray,
To meet the unexpected.

Perhaps some loss may come to me,
Some care, or some perplexity,
Then He my strength and stay shall be
To face the unexpected.

How oft within the trivial round
So many trying things are found;
But he can make all grace abound
For all the unexpected.

No matter what the call may be,
Or changes that may come to me;
His hand of love in all I see
From sources unexpected.
ANONYMOUS

One thing God has spoken,
*   two things have I heard:*
That you, O God, are strong,
*   and that you, O Lord, are loving.*
PSALM 62:11-12

*T*he love of God is the ultimate reality, the deepest and strongest force in the universe.

DAVID SMITH

When life gets crazy, you need something to grip. Here are the truths about God that keep me in the saddle:

> God is in control.
> He leads me along a path he has planned.
> Nothing can touch me that is not in his plan.
> He's passionate about my highest good.
> His grace is available and abundant.

My trials are not forever. He will lead me through, and an end is in sight. These are the strands that weave the strong rope of truth. As long as I hang on, I will never despair.

THE ROSE

I am a rose of Sharon,
a lily of the valleys.
SONG OF SONGS 2:1

Some people claim that the rose is the crown jewel of the garden. It's one of my favorites, and I enjoy capturing its intricacies with paint and brush. For all these reasons and more, I was touched by a poem sent to me a couple of years ago. Written by a missionary, it's called "The Rose."

It's only a tiny rosebud—
a flower of God's design;
But I can't unfold the petals
with these clumsy hands of mine.
The secret of unfolding flowers
is not known to such as I—
The flower God opens so sweetly
in my hands would fade and die.
If I cannot unfold a rosebud
this flower of God's design,
Then how can I think I have wisdom
to unfold this life of mine?
So I'll trust in Him for His leading
each moment of every day,
And I'll look to Him for His guidance
each step of the pilgrim way.
For the pathway that lies before me
my Heavenly Father knows—
I'll trust Him to unfold the moments
just as He unfolds the rose.

As the poem suggests, we can't grow the moments of our lives any more than we can peel back the petals of a rose. We look to God's leading each moment of the day, we can trust him to unfurl each hour just as he unfurls the rose. Little wonder the Lord is called the Rose of Sharon. We just can't get enough of watching his glory, like that glorious flower, unfold in our lives.

*Lord, your love for me is as beautiful as a rose
that is just beginning to bloom. May I stand back
and watch in awe as you unfold this life of mine
and make all parts of it absolutely exquisite.*

*If I rise on the wings of the dawn,
if I settle on the far side of the sea,
even there your hand will guide me, Lord,
your right hand will hold me fast.
If I say, "Surely the darkness will hide me
and the light become night around me,"
even the darkness will not be dark to you;
the night will shine like the day,
for darkness is as light to you.*

PSALM 139:9-12

BOLD LOVE

Jesus entered Jericho and was passing through. A man was there by the name of Zacchaeus; he was a chief tax collector and was wealthy. He wanted to see who Jesus was, but being a short man he could not, because of the crowd. So he ran ahead and climbed a sycamore-fig tree to see him, since Jesus was coming that way. When Jesus reached the spot, he looked up and said to him, "Zacchaeus, come down immediately. I must stay at your house today." So he came down at once and welcomed him gladly.

LUKE 19:1-6

Why it is that Jesus singled out the little man in the sycamore tree, no one knows. But what is clear is this: The Lord stepped boldly into Zacchaeus's life. Out of the entire crowd, Jesus called him by name. He told Zacchaeus to scurry down from his perch. And the Lord not only invited Himself to his home, He hardly gave the little man time to think twice about it.

Some would say that Jesus was a bit bold to presume upon Zacchaeus. *Telling* a host he must open his home to you? Bold, yes. But it was the boldness of love. Jesus ensured that His command would be well received, for He inclined the heart of Zacchaeus to welcome Him.

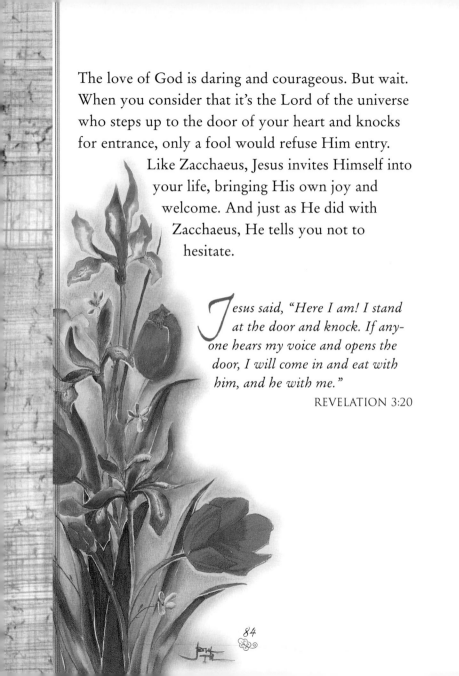

The love of God is daring and courageous. But wait. When you consider that it's the Lord of the universe who steps up to the door of your heart and knocks for entrance, only a fool would refuse Him entry.

Like Zacchaeus, Jesus invites Himself into your life, bringing His own joy and welcome. And just as He did with Zacchaeus, He tells you not to hesitate.

Jesus said, "Here I am! I stand at the door and knock. If anyone hears my voice and opens the door, I will come in and eat with him, and he with me."

REVELATION 3:20

Lord, thank you for your daring and courageous love for me. Help me throw open the door of my heart to You and say, "Welcome!"

"*Let us acknowledge the LORD;*
  let us press on to acknowledge him
As surely as the sun rises,
he will appear;
he will come to us like the winter rains,
like the spring rains that water the earth."

HOSEA 6:3

IN HIS HAND

We're in his hand, that mighty hand,
      that flung the universe in space,
That guides the sun and moon and stars,
      and holds the planets in their place.
We're in that hand, that skillful hand,
      that made the blinded eyes to see,
That touched the leper, cleansed and healed,
      and set the palsied sufferer free.

We're in that hand, that living hand,
      that lifted children to his breast,
That fed the hungry multitudes
      and beckoned weary hearts to rest.
We're in his hands, those pierced hands,
      once nailed to Calvary's cruel tree,
Where there in agony and blood
      he paid the price to set us free.

ANONYMOUS

This is how God showed his love among us: He sent his one and only Son into the world that we might live through him.

1 JOHN 4:9

*I*f all of God's love could be expressed in one word, that word would be Jesus.

CONOVER SWOFFORD

*J*esus said, *"Love each other as I have loved you.*
Greater love has no man than this, that he lay down
his life for his friends."

JOHN 15:12-13

*G*ive thanks to the Lord, call on his name;
make known among the nations what he has done.

1 CHRONICLES 16:8

*J*n the same way, let your light shine before men, that
they may see your good deeds and praise your Father
in heaven.

MATTHEW 5:16

GOD'S OMIAGES

Every good and perfect gift is from above,
coming down from the Father of the heavenly
lights, who does not change.
JAMES 1:17

Some gifts you give because it's expected. Other gifts are spur-of-the-moment surprises. Such are the gifts Ken enjoys presenting to me. He calls them *omiages*. In Japanese, it means "a little gift that you are not required to give, as for a special occasion."

When I'm on a trip, I have fun picking out omiages for my husband. Once it was a tie from Ohio, another time it was a T-shirt from New York City. When I came home from Texas, I presented him with a jar of chili sauce. Little, unexpected gifts. Ken is always so pleased because he knows that an omiage doesn't have to be given. That makes it all the more special.

That's the way Jesus is with us. He's not obligated to give us gifts. He's not required to shower us with blessings. He owes this utterly rebellious planet absolutely nothing, and that's why His gifts are all the more special.

God gives gifts simply because He wants to. To top it off, they are generous gifts, not little omiages, but big ones!

Lord and Giver of Life, thank you for being so generous. Today I will count my blessings and be mindful to turn to You often and say, "Thank you!"

SHOUT LOUDER!

*D*o you go through dry times in prayer when you would swear God wasn't listening—or that he was preoccupied over some global crisis? I confess I do.

Meditations are sometimes barren and seem to yield no fruit. But even Teresa of Avila acknowledged that in every 15 minutes of prayer there are 14 minutes of distraction.

During such times, please remember that God is not busy or taking a snooze. His love is changeless and constant. His purpose for you is still on course. True, there may be times when he leads you through a stretch of dry wasteland, when his joys aren't as evident, but remember that even the Israelites who wandered in the desert for 40 years were—the whole time—actually only a few days' journey from the promised land!

*J*esus answered, *"In that day you will no longer ask me anything. I tell you the truth, my Father will give you whatever you ask in my name. Until now you have not asked for anything in my name. Ask and you will receive, and your joy will be complete.*

JOHN 16: 23-24

*D*o not be anxious about anything, but in everything, by prayer and petition, with thanksgiving, present your requests to God.
And the peace of God, which transcends all understanding, will guard your hearts and your minds in Christ Jesus.

PHILIPPIANS 4: 6-7

LOVING THROUGH THE TOUGH TIMES

I grieve to think how I treated my friends when I was in the hospital. They would sit by my bedside while I lay there in stubborn silence. They would bring magazines, and I would say I wasn't interested. I'm sure that I provoked my friends to exasperation. A few stopped coming around and who could blame them?

We sometimes feel that way about God. Deep down we know we probably provoke God with our sloppy prayers and ho-hum approach to Bible study. We're certain that he's irritated with our sins and annoyed with our constant ups and downs. We assume he must be exasperated to the point that he will "stop coming around."

Yet if we are truly God's children, we can be sure that he will love us right through the tough times. Children can be exasperating—even children of God—but the Lord will never give up on us. Nothing will be able to separate us from God's constant and abiding love (Romans 8:39).

Lord, thank you for always being around-even when I have been tough to deal with. Thank you for loving me no matter what.

Excerpts taken from these books by Joni Eareckson Tada:

More Precious Than Silver. Grand Rapids, MI: Zondervan, 1998.

Secret Strength. Sisters, OR: Multnomah Books, 1994.

Diamonds in the Dust. Grand Rapids, MI: Zondervan, 1993.

NIV Encouragement Bible. With Dave and Jan Dravecky. Grand Rapids, MI: Zondervan, 2001.

Material also taken from:

God's Love to Encourage You. Grand Rapids, MI: Zondervan, 1997

Komp, Diane M.: Bedtime Snacks for the Soul. Grand Rapids, MI: Zondervan, 2000.

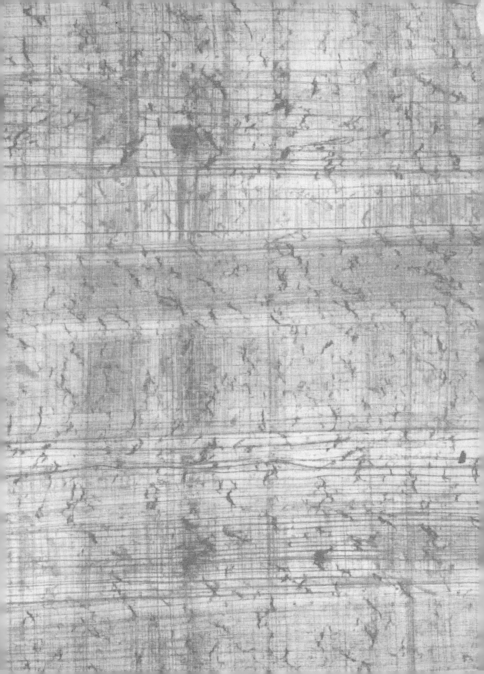